FORTY LITTLE PIECES

In Progressive Order for Beginner Flutists

BY BACH · HANDEL · HAYDN · MOZART · BEETHOVEN · SCHUBERT · SCHUMANN

Transcribed and Adapted for
Flute and Piano by Louis Moyse

ISBN 978-0-7935-2552-2

G. SCHIRMER, Inc.

DISTRIBUTED BY

HAL•LEONARD®
CORPORATION

7777 W. BLUEMOUND RD. P.O. BOX 13819 MILWAUKEE, WI 53213

CONTENTS

Forty Little Pieces
in Progressive Order
for Beginner Flutists

Transcribed and adapted by
Louis Moyse

1. Ah! Vous dirai-je, maman

W. A. Mozart

43917CX

2. Little Piece

R. Schumann

3. Gavotte

J. S. Bach

4. Humming Song

R. Schumann

5. Menuet

G. F. Handel

Allegretto con moto ♩ = c. 108

43917

6. Melody

R. Schumann

8

7. Menuet

J. S. Bach

43917

8. Soldier's March

R. Schumann

43917

9. Scotch Dance

L. van Beethoven

10. About Strange Lands and People

R. Schumann

11. Waltz

F. Schubert

12. Minuet

W. A. Mozart

13. Aria

G. F. Handel

14. Arietta

F. J. Haydn

15. Ariette

W. A. Mozart

16. Little Dance

F. J. Haydn

43917

17. Andante

F. Schubert

18. Gavotte

G. F. Handel

43917

19. Minuetto

L. van Beethoven

20. Minuet

W. A. Mozart

43917

21. Country Dance

F. Schubert

22. Menuet

J. S. Bach

43917

23. The Reaper's Song

R. Schumann

Not very fast ♩.=c.76

FORTY LITTLE PIECES

Transcribed and Adapted for
Flute and Piano by Louis Moyse

FLUTE

In Progressive Order
for Beginner Flutists

CONTENTS

ISBN 978-0-7935-2552-2

G. SCHIRMER, Inc.

DISTRIBUTED BY
HAL•LEONARD®
CORPORATION
7777 W. BLUEMOUND RD. P.O. BOX 13819 MILWAUKEE, WI 53213

Forty Little Pieces

in Progressive Order

for Beginner Flutists

Flute

Transcribed and adapted by
Louis Moyse

1. Ah! Vous dirai-je, maman

W. A. Mozart

2. Little Piece

R. Schumann

3. Gavotte

J. S. Bach

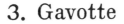

4. Humming Song

R. Schumann

5. Menuet

G. F. Handel

6. Melody

R. Schumann

7. Menuet

J. S. Bach

8. Soldier's March

R. Schumann

9. Scotch Dance

L. van Beethoven

10. About Strange Lands and People

R. Schumann

11. Waltz

F. Schubert

12. Minuet

W. A. Mozart

Flute

13. Aria

G. F. Handel

Andantino ♩ = c. 108

14. Arietta

F. J. Haydn

Allegretto ♩ = c. 112

15. Ariette

W. A. Mozart

16. Little Dance

F. J. Haydn

43917

17. Andante

F. Schubert

18. Gavotte

G. F. Handel

19. Minuetto

L. van Beethoven

20. Minuet

W. A. Mozart

Trio

43917

21. Country Dance

F. Schubert

22. Menuet

J. S. Bach

43917

23. The Reaper's Song

R. Schumann

Not very fast ♩.=c.76

24. Little Piece

F. J. Haydn

Andantino un poco allegretto ♩=c.112

43917

25. Menuet of Mr. Duport

W. A. Mozart

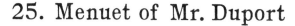

Tempo di menuetto ♩=c.104

26. Menuet

F. Schubert

♩=c.112

Trio

27. Andante

F. J. Haydn

28. Adieu to the Piano

Attributed to
L. van Beethoven

Moderato con molto espressione ♩= c. 104

29. Allegro

W. A. Mozart

30. March

J. S. Bach

31. Allegro

F. J. Haydn

32. Polonaise

J. S. Bach

33. Menuetto

G. F. Handel

34. Gavotte

J. S. Bach

35. Andantino

F. Schubert

36. Moment Musicale

F. Schubert

Allegro moderato ♩ = c. 84

37. Musette

J. S. Bach

38. Bourrée

G. F. Handel

39. Sonatina

I

L. van Beethoven

Moderato ♩= c. 126

Romanze

II

♩. = c. 72

poco rit. a tempo

40. Serenade

F. J. Haydn

24. Little Piece

F. J. Haydn

43917

25. Menuet of Mr. Duport

W. A. Mozart

Tempo di menuetto ♩= c.104

26. Menuet

F. Schubert

Trio

43917

27. Andante

F. J. Haydn

43917

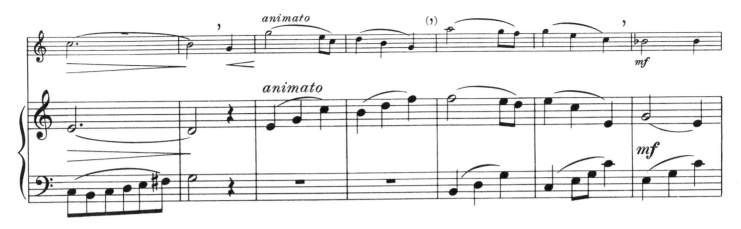

43917

28. Adieu to the Piano

Attributed to
L. van Beethoven

Moderato, con molto espressione ♩= c.104

Trio

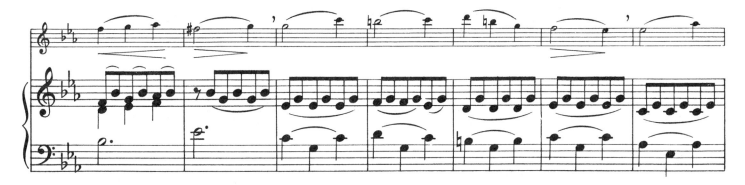

29. Allegro

W. A. Mozart

30. March

J.S. Bach

31. Allegro

F. J. Haydn

43917

32. Polonaise

J. S. Bach

43917

33. Menuetto

G. F. Handel

43917

34. Gavotte

J. S. Bach

35. Andantino

F. Schubert

43917

36. Moment Musical

F. Schubert

Allegro moderato ♩ = c. 84

43917

43917

37. Musette

J. S. Bach

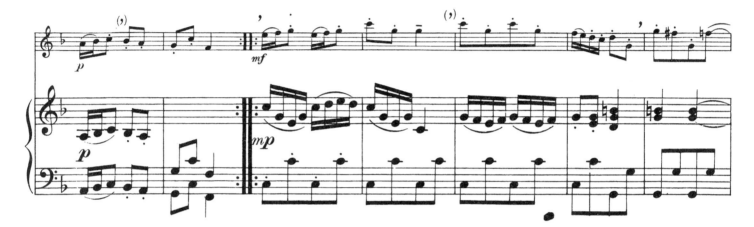

38. Bourrée

G. F. Handel

39. Sonatina

I

L. van Beethoven

Romanze

II

43917

43917

40. Serenade

F. J. Haydn

43917

49